1. *Omit "00" in the cents columns.*

Income Statement

For Year Ended December 31, 19—

2. *Omit "00" in the cents columns.*

Statement of Owner's Equity

For Year Ended December 31, 19—

			Total

3. *Omit "00" in the cents columns.*

	Balance Sheet					
	December 31, 19—					

Page not used.

1. *Omit "00" in the cents columns.*

PROBLEM 14 - 6 ___

GRAY, HALE, AND IVES
Statement of Partnership Liquidation
For Period December 1-20, 19—

	CASH	NONCASH ASSETS	LIABILITIES	CAPITAL GRAY (50%)	HALE (30%)	IVES (20%)
Balances before realization	15400	87100	50000	30400	8000	14100
Sale of assets and division of loss	+37100	-87100	---	-25000	-15000	-10000
Balances after realization	52500	0	50000	5400	7000 (Dr)	4100
Payment of liabilities	-50000	---	-50000	---	---	---
Balances after payment of liabilities	2500	0	0	5400	7000 (Dr)	4100
Receipt (Division) of deficiency						
Balances						
Distribution of cash to partners						
Final balances						

2.

JOURNAL   PAGE

	DATE		DESCRIPTION	POST. REF.	DEBIT	CREDIT	
1							1
2							2
3							3
4							4
5							5
6							6
7							7
8							8
9							9
10							10
11							11
12							12
13							13
14							14
15							15
16							16
17							17
18							18
19							19
20							20
21							21
22							22
23							23
24							24
25							25
26							26
27							27
28							28
29							29
30							30
31							31
32							32

1. Omit "00" in the cents columns.

Statement of Partnership Liquidation
For Period

	CASH	NONCASH ASSETS	LIABILITIES	CAPITAL		
Balances before realization						

2. Omit "00" in the cents columns.

Statement of Partnership Liquidation
For Period

	CASH	NONCASH ASSETS	LIABILITIES	CAPITAL		
Balances before realization						

3. Omit "00" in the cents columns.

Statement of Partnership Liquidation
For Period

	CASH	NONCASH ASSETS	LIABILITIES	CAPITAL		
Balances before realization						

Page not used.

1. *Omit "00" in the cents columns.*

	LEWIS	MEYER	TOTAL
NET INCOME, $200,000			

	LEWIS	MEYER	TOTAL
NET INCOME, $140,000			

	LEWIS	MEYER	TOTAL
NET INCOME, $100,000			

2.

3.

1.

JOURNAL

PAGE

	DATE		DESCRIPTION	POST. REF.	DEBIT	CREDIT	
1							1
2							2
3							3
4							4
5							5
6							6
7							7
8							8
9							9
10							10
11							11
12							12
13							13
14							14
15							15
16							16
17							17
18							18
19							19
20							20
21							21
22							22
23							23
24							24
25							25
26							26
27							27
28							28
29							29
30							30
31							31
32							32

2. *Omit "00" in the cents columns.*

Stockholders' Equity

Note to Students: The completion of these T accounts is not required by the problem, but may be an aid in preparing the stockholders' equity section of the balance sheet.

Preferred Stock

Paid-In Capital in Excess of Par — Preferred Stock

Common Stock

Paid-In Capital in Excess of Par — Common Stock

Retained Earnings

Page not used.

1.

JOURNAL

	DATE		DESCRIPTION	POST. REF.	DEBIT	CREDIT	
1							1
2							2
3							3
4							4
5							5
6							6
7							7
8							8
9							9
10							10
11							11
12							12
13							13
14							14
15							15
16							16
17							17
18							18
19							19
20							20
21							21
22							22
23							23
24							24
25							25
26							26
27							27
28							28
29							29
30							30
31							31
32							32

PROBLEM 15 - 4 ___ , Continued

2. *Omit "00" in the cents columns.*

Stockholders' Equity

Note to Students: The completion of these T accounts is not required by the problem, but may be an aid in preparing the stockholders' equity section of the balance sheet.

Preferred Stock Subscriptions Receivable

Preferred Stock

Preferred Stock Subscribed

Paid-In Capital in Excess of Par — Preferred Stock

Common Stock

Paid-In Capital in Excess of Par — Common Stock

Treasury Stock

Paid-In Capital from Sale of Treasury Stock

Retained Earnings

1.

JOURNAL

PAGE _____

	DATE		DESCRIPTION	POST. REF.	DEBIT	CREDIT	
1							1
2							2
3							3
4							4
5							5
6							6
7							7
8							8
9							9
10							10
11							11
12							12
13							13
14							14
15							15
16							16
17							17
18							18
19							19
20							20
21							21
22							22
23							23
24							24
25							25
26							26
27							27
28							28
29							29
30							30
31							31
32							32

2. Omit "00" in the cents columns.

Work Sheet

December 31, 19—

ACCOUNT TITLE	BALANCES PER BALANCE SHEET		CORRECTIONS		CORRECTED BALANCES	
	DEBIT	CREDIT	DEBIT	CREDIT	DEBIT	CREDIT
1 Cash						
2 Accounts Receivable						
3 Merchandise Inventory						
4 Prepaid Insurance						
5 Treasury Common Stock						
6 Equipment						
7 Retained Earnings						
8						
9 Accounts Payable						
10 Preferred Stock						
11 Common Stock						
12 Paid-In Cap. in Excess of Par—						
13 Common Stock						
14						
15						
16						
17						
18						
19						
20						
21						
22						
23						
24						
25						

3. *Omit "00" in the cents columns.*

Balance Sheet

December 31, 19—

PROBLEM 15 - 6 ___ , Concluded

4.

CLASS OF STOCK	TOTAL EQUITY ALLOCATED	NUMBER OF SHARES	EQUITY PER SHARE	

Page not used.

1. and 2.

Omit "00" in the cents columns.

Retained Earnings Statement											
For Year Ended December 31, 19—											

Page not used.

1. and 2.

Common Stock

Paid-In Capital in Excess of Par — Common Stock

Appropriation for Bonded Indebtedness

Retained Earnings

Treasury Stock

Paid-In Capital from Sale of Treasury Stock

Donated Capital

Cash Dividends

Stock Dividends

Stock Dividends Distributable

2.

JOURNAL

PAGE _____

	DATE		DESCRIPTION	POST. REF.	DEBIT	CREDIT	
1							1
2							2
3							3
4							4
5							5
6							6
7							7
8							8
9							9
10							10
11							11
12							12
13							13
14							14
15							15
16							16
17							17
18							18
19							19
20							20
21							21
22							22
23							23
24							24
25							25
26							26
27							27
28							28
29							29
30							30
31							31
32							32

PROBLEM 16 - 5 ___ , Continued

JOURNAL

PAGE

	DATE		DESCRIPTION	POST. REF.	DEBIT	CREDIT	
1							1
2							2
3							3
4							4
5							5
6							6
7							7
8							8
9							9
10							10
11							11
12							12
13							13
14							14
15							15
16							16
17							17
18							18
19							19
20							20
21							21
22							22
23							23
24							24
25							25
26							26
27							27
28							28
29							29
30							30
31							31
32							32

3. *Omit "00" in the cents columns.*

Stockholders' Equity

PROBLEM 16 - 5 ___ , Concluded

4. *Omit "00" in the cents columns.*

Retained Earnings Statement

For Year Ended December 31, 19—

1.

JOURNAL

	DATE		DESCRIPTION	POST. REF.	DEBIT	CREDIT	
1							1
2							2
3							3
4							4
5							5
6							6
7							7
8							8
9							9
10							10
11							11
12							12
13							13
14							14
15							15
16							16
17							17
18							18
19							19
20							20
21							21
22							22
23							23
24							24
25							25
26							26
27							27
28							28
29							29
30							30
31							31
32							32

2. *Omit "00" in the cents columns.*

Income Statement
For Year Ended December 31, 19—

Name _____

PROBLEM 16 - 7 ___ , Continued

3. *Omit "00" in the cents columns.*

Retained Earnings Statement

For Year Ended December 31, 19—

4. *Omit "00" in the cents columns.*

	Balance Sheet
	December 31, 19—

Name _____

JOURNAL
PAGE

	DATE		DESCRIPTION	POST. REF.	DEBIT	CREDIT	
1							1
2							2
3							3
4							4
5							5
6							6
7							7
8							8
9							9
10							10
11							11
12							12
13							13
14							14
15							15
16							16
17							17
18							18
19							19
20							20
21							21
22							22
23							23
24							24
25							25
26							26
27							27
28							28
29							29
30							30
31							31
32							32

JOURNAL

PAGE

	DATE		DESCRIPTION	POST. REF.	DEBIT	CREDIT	
1							1
2							2
3							3
4							4
5							5
6							6
7							7
8							8
9							9
10							10
11							11
12							12
13							13
14							14
15							15
16							16
17							17
18							18
19							19
20							20
21							21
22							22
23							23
24							24
25							25
26							26
27							27
28							28
29							29
30							30
31							31
32							32

1. and 2. _____

1.

	Plan 1	Plan 2	Plan 3
Earnings before interest and income tax			
Deduct interest on bonds			
Income before income tax			
Deduct income tax			
Net income			
Dividends on preferred stock			
Available for dividends on common stock			
Shares of common stock outstanding			
Earnings per share on common stock			

2.

	Plan 1	Plan 2	Plan 3
Earnings before interest and income tax			
Deduct interest on bonds			
Income before income tax			
Deduct income tax			
Net income			
Dividends on preferred stock			
Available for dividends on common stock			
Shares of common stock outstanding			
Earnings per share on common stock			

3.

Name _____

PROBLEM 17 - 2 ___

1., 2. and 3.

JOURNAL

PAGE _____

	DATE		DESCRIPTION	POST. REF.	DEBIT	CREDIT	
1							1
2							2
3							3
4							4
5							5
6							6
7							7
8							8
9							9
10							10
11							11
12							12
13							13
14							14
15							15
16							16
17							17
18							18
19							19
20							20
21							21
22							22
23							23
24							24
25							25
26							26
27							27
28							28
29							29
30							30
31							31
32							32

JOURNAL

PAGE

	DATE		DESCRIPTION	POST. REF.	DEBIT	CREDIT	
1							1
2							2
3							3
4							4
5							5
6							6
7							7
8							8
9							9
10							10
11							11
12							12
13							13
14							14
15							15
16							16
17							17
18							18
19							19

4. _____

_____

_____

_____

_____

5. _____

_____

_____

_____

_____

_____

_____

_____

1.

JOURNAL

PAGE _____

	DATE		DESCRIPTION	POST. REF.	DEBIT	CREDIT	
1							1
2							2
3							3
4							4
5							5
6							6
7							7
8							8
9							9
10							10
11							11
12							12
13							13
14							14
15							15
16							16
17							17
18							18
19							19
20							20
21							21
22							22
23							23
24							24
25							25
26							26
27							27
28							28
29							29
30							30
31							31
32							32

JOURNAL

PAGE

	DATE	DESCRIPTION	POST. REF.	DEBIT	CREDIT	
1						1
2						2
3						3
4						4
5						5
6						6
7						7
8						8
9						9
10						10
11						11
12						12
13						13
14						14
15						15
16						16
17						17
18						18
19						19
20						20
21						21
22						22
23						23

2.

Year	Bond Interest Expense for Year	Sinking Fund Income for Year	Account Balances at End of Year				
			Bonds Payable	____ on Bonds	Sinking Fund		Appro-priation for B.I.
					Cash	Investments	
1994							
1995							

1.

JOURNAL   PAGE _____

	DATE		DESCRIPTION	POST. REF.	DEBIT	CREDIT	
1							1
2							2
3							3
4							4
5							5
6							6
7							7
8							8
9							9
10							10
11							11
12							12
13							13
14							14
15							15
16							16
17							17
18							18
19							19
20							20
21							21
22							22
23							23
24							24
25							25
26							26
27							27
28							28
29							29
30							30
31							31
32							32

JOURNAL

PAGE

	DATE	DESCRIPTION	POST. REF.	DEBIT	CREDIT	
1						1
2						2
3						3
4						4
5						5
6						6
7						7
8						8
9						9
10						10
11						11
12						12
13						13
14						14
15						15
16						16
17						17
18						18
19						19
20						20
21						21
22						22
23						23
24						24
25						25

2. a. $ _____

    b. $ _____

3. _____ %

    Computations: _____

    _____

    _____

4. _____

    _____

    _____

    _____

Name _____

1.

	Plan 1	Plan 2

2. _____

Name _____

1.

JOURNAL

PAGE _____

	DATE		DESCRIPTION	POST. REF.	DEBIT	CREDIT	
1							1
2							2
3							3
4							4
5							5
6							6
7							7
8							8
9							9
10							10
11							11
12							12
13							13
14							14
15							15
16							16
17							17
18							18
19							19
20							20
21							21
22							22
23							23
24							24
25							25
26							26
27							27
28							28
29							29
30							30
31							31
32							32

JOURNAL

PAGE

	DATE		DESCRIPTION	POST. REF.	DEBIT	CREDIT	
1							1
2							2
3							3
4							4
5							5
6							6
7							7
8							8
9							9
10							10
11							11
12							12
13							13
14							14
15							15
16							16
17							17
18							18
19							19
20							20
21							21
22							22
23							23
24							24
25							25
26							26
27							27
28							28
29							29
30							30
31							31
32							32

JOURNAL

	DATE		DESCRIPTION	POST. REF.	DEBIT	CREDIT	
1							1
2							2
3							3
4							4
5							5
6							6
7							7
8							8
9							9
10							10
11							11
12							12
13							13
14							14
15							15
16							16
17							17
18							18
19							19
20							20
21							21
22							22
23							23
24							24
25							25
26							26
27							27
28							28
29							29
30							30
31							31
32							32

COMPREHENSIVE PROBLEM 5, Continued

JOURNAL

PAGE

	DATE		DESCRIPTION	POST. REF.	DEBIT	CREDIT	
1							1
2							2
3							3
4							4
5							5
6							6
7							7
8							8
9							9
10							10
11							11
12							12
13							13
14							14
15							15
16							16
17							17
18							18
19							19
20							20
21							21
22							22
23							23
24							24
25							25
26							26
27							27
28							28
29							29
30							30
31							31
32							32

2. a. *Omit "00" in the cents columns.*

WALTON INC.

Income Statement

For Year Ended March 31, 1994

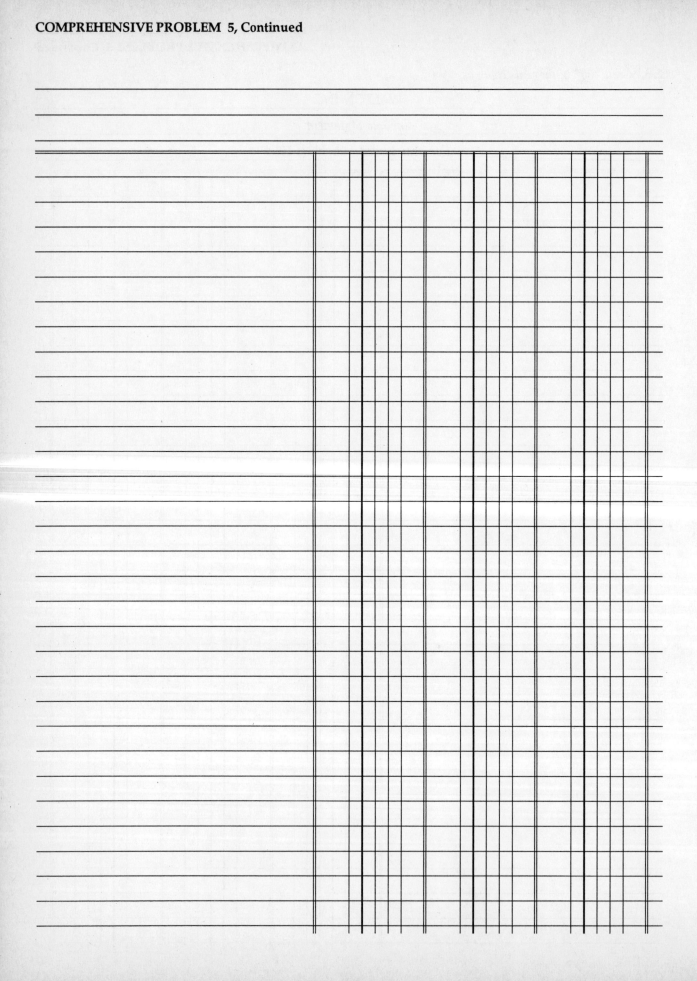

2.b. *Omit "00" in the cents columns.*

WALTON INC.

Retained Earnings Statement

For Year Ended March 31, 1994

COMPREHENSIVE PROBLEM 5, Continued

2.c. *Omit "00" in the cents columns.*

WALTON INC.

Balance Sheet

March 31, 1994

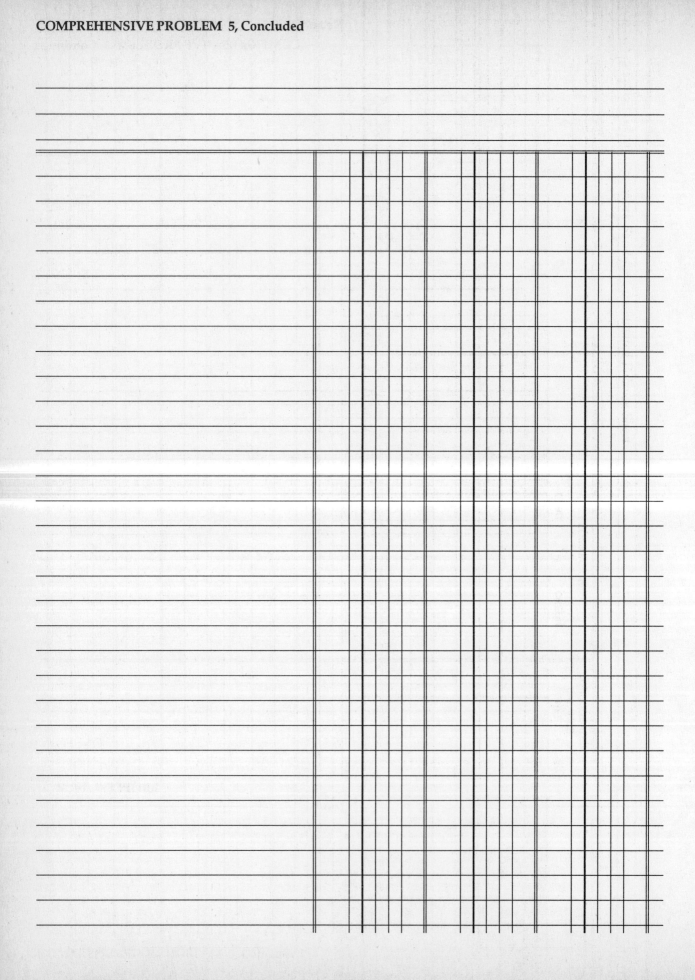

1. a.

JOURNAL

PAGE _____

	DATE		DESCRIPTION	POST. REF.	DEBIT	CREDIT	
1							1
2							2
3							3
4							4
5							5

b. *Omit "00" in the cents columns.*

Consolidated Balance Sheet

	DEBIT		CREDIT	

This work sheet is not required, but may be used in completing the requirements of the problem.

1. b.

Work Sheet for Consolidated Balance Sheet

	ELIMINATIONS		CONSOLIDATED BALANCE SHEET
	DEBIT	CREDIT	

2. a.

JOURNAL

PAGE _____

	DATE		DESCRIPTION	POST. REF.	DEBIT	CREDIT	
1							1
2							2
3							3
4							4
5							5

b. *Omit "00" in the cents columns.*

Consolidated Balance Sheet

This work sheet is not required, but may be used in completing the requirements of the problem.

2. b.

Work Sheet for Consolidated Balance Sheet

		ELIMINATIONS		CONSOLIDATED BALANCE SHEET
		DEBIT	CREDIT	

3. *Omit "00" in the cents columns.*

Consolidated Balance Sheet

1. *Eliminations:* _____

   a. _____

   b. _____

   c. _____

   d. _____

3. *Eliminations:* _____

   a. _____

   b. _____

   c. _____

4. *Omit "00" in the cents columns.*

Consolidated Income Statement
For Year Ended December 31, 19—

5. Reduction in consolidated inventories, net income, and retained earnings: $ _____

2. *Omit "00" in the cents columns.*

Consolidated Balance Sheet

December 31, 19—

Name _____

Omit "00" in the cents columns.

Consolidated Balance Sheet

This work sheet is not required, but may be used in completing the requirements of the problem.

Work Sheet for Consolidated Balance Sheet

			CONSOLIDATED BALANCE SHEET
	ELIMINATIONS	CREDIT	
		DEBIT	

	CONSOLIDATED BALANCE SHEET	ELIMINATIONS						
		CREDIT	DEBIT					

Omit "00" in the cents columns.

Consolidated Balance Sheet

1. and 2.

JOURNAL

	DATE		DESCRIPTION	POST. REF.	DEBIT	CREDIT	
1							1
2							2
3							3
4							4
5							5
6							6
7							7
8							8
9							9
10							10
11							11
12							12
13							13
14							14
15							15
16							16
17							17
18							18
19							19
20							20
21							21
22							22
23							23
24							24
25							25
26							26
27							27
28							28
29							29
30							30
31							31
32							32

JOURNAL

PAGE

	DATE		DESCRIPTION	POST. REF.	DEBIT	CREDIT	
1							1
2							2
3							3
4							4
5							5
6							6
7							7
8							8
9							9
10							10
11							11
12							12
13							13
14							14
15							15
16							16
17							17
18							18
19							19
20							20
21							21
22							22
23							23
24							24
25							25
26							26
27							27
28							28
29							29
30							30
31							31
32							32
33							33

1. and 2.

Omit "00" in the cents columns.

<table>
<tr><td colspan="2" align="center">*Statement of Cash Flows*</td></tr>
<tr><td colspan="2" align="center">*For Year Ended*</td></tr>
</table>

The use of this form is not required unless so indicated by the instructor.

Work Sheet for Statement of Cash Flows
For Year Ended

ACCOUNTS	BALANCE, _____, 1993	TRANSACTIONS		BALANCE, _____, 1994
		DEBIT	CREDIT	

Omit "00" in the cents columns.

Statement of Cash Flows

For Year Ended _____

The use of this form is not required unless so indicated by the instructor.

Work Sheet for Statement of Cash Flows
For Year Ended

ACCOUNTS	BALANCE, _____ , 1993	TRANSACTIONS		BALANCE, _____ , 1994
		DEBIT	CREDIT	

Name _____

Omit "00" in the cents columns.

Statement of Cash Flows					
For Year Ended December 31, 1994					

The use of this form is not required unless so indicated by the instructor.

Work Sheet for Statement of Cash Flows
For Year Ended December 31, 1994

ACCOUNTS	BALANCE, DEC. 31, 1993	TRANSACTIONS		BALANCE, DEC. 31, 1994
		DEBIT	CREDIT	

Omit "00" in the cents columns.

Statement of Cash Flows

For Year Ended December 31, 1994

PROBLEM 19 - 5 ___ , Continued

Name _____

The use of this form is not required unless so indicated by the instructor.

Work Sheet for Statement of Cash Flows
For Year Ended December 31, 1994

ACCOUNTS	BALANCE, DEC. 31, 1993	TRANSACTIONS		BALANCE, DEC. 31, 1994
		DEBIT	CREDIT	

Omit "00" in the cents columns.

Statement of Cash Flows

For Year Ended December 31, 1994

Name _____

PROBLEM 19 - 6 ___ , Continued

542

The use of this form is not required unless so indicated by the instructor.

Work Sheet for Statement of Cash Flows
For Year Ended December 31, 1994

ACCOUNTS	BALANCE, DEC. 31, 1993	TRANSACTIONS		BALANCE, DEC. 31, 1994
		DEBIT	CREDIT	

1. and 2. _____

1.

Comparative Income Statement
For Years Ended

	19___	19___	INCREASE (DECREASE*)	
			AMOUNT	PERCENT

2.

1.

Comparative Income Statement
For Years Ended

	19____		19____	
	AMOUNT	PERCENT	AMOUNT	PERCENT

2.

Name _____

PROBLEM 20 - 3 ___

1.

Common-Size Income Statement
For Year Ended December 31, 19—

	PUBLISHING COMPANY	PUBLISHING INDUSTRY AVERAGE

2.

1.a.

1.b.

1.c.

2.

Transaction	Working Capital	Current Ratio	Acid-Test Ratio
a.			
b.			
c.			
d.			
e.			
f.			
g.			
h.			
i.			
j.			

1.a. _____

_____

_____

_____

_____

_____

_____

1.b. _____

_____

_____

_____

_____

1.c. _____

_____

_____

_____

_____

_____

_____

3.

Error	Working Capital	Current Ratio	Acid-Test Ratio
a.			
b.			
c.			
d.			
e.			
f.			
g.			
h.			

2.

JOURNAL

	DATE		DESCRIPTION	POST. REF.	DEBIT	CREDIT	
1							1
2							2
3							3
4							4
5							5
6							6
7							7
8							8
9							9
10							10
11							11
12							12
13							13
14							14
15							15
16							16
17							17
18							18
19							19
20							20
21							21
22							22
23							23
24							24
25							25
26							26
27							27
28							28
29							29
30							30
31							31
32							32

4.

Schedule of Working Capital

5.

1. through 18. _____

Name _____

Name _____

Comparative Income Statement
For Years Ended

	1994		1993	
	AMOUNT	PERCENT	AMOUNT	PERCENT

1. _____

2.

1. *Omit "00" in the cents columns.*

MALONE COMPANY

Statement of Cash Flows

For Year Ended December 31, 1994

2. *Omit "00" in the cents columns.*

MALONE COMPANY

Statement of Cash Flows

For Year Ended December 31, 1994

3.

a. _____

b. _____

c. _____

d. _____

e. _____

f. _____

g. _____

h. _____

i. _____

j. _____

k. _____

l. _____

m. _____

n. _____

o. _____

p. _____

q. _____

r. _____

s. _____

t. _____

u. _____

v. _____

w. _____

_____

_____

_____

_____

_____

_____

_____

_____

_____

_____

_____

Page not used.

Case One

a. _____

b. _____

c. _____

d. _____

e. _____

Case Two

a. _____

b. _____

c. _____

d. _____

e. _____

Case Three

a. _____

b. _____

c. _____

d. _____

e. _____

Case Four

a. _____

b. _____

c. _____

d. _____

e. _____

Case Five

a. _____

b. _____

c. _____

d. _____

e. _____

Page not used.

1.

2.

Cost	Variable Cost		Fixed Cost	
	Direct Cost	Indirect Cost	Direct Cost	Indirect Cost
a.				
b.				
c.				
d.				
e.				
f.				
g.				
h.				
i.				
j.				
k.				
l.				
m.				
n.				
o.				
p.				
q.				
r.				
s.				
t.				
u.				
v.				
w.				
x.				
y.				
z.				

Page not used.

	Product Cost			Period Cost	
Cost	Direct Materials Cost	Direct Labor Cost	Factory Overhead Cost	Selling Expense	Administrative Expense
a.					
b.					
c.					
d.					
e.					
f.					
g.					
h.					
i.					
j.					
k.					
l.					
m.					
n.					
o.					
p.					
q.					
r.					
s.					
t.					
u.					
v.					
w.					
x.					
y.					
z.					

Page not used.

Cost	Product Cost			Period Cost	
	Direct Materials Cost	Direct Labor Cost	Factory Overhead Cost	Selling Expense	Administrative Expense
a.					
b.					
c.					
d.					
e.					
f.					
g.					
h.					
i.					
j.					
k.					
l.					
m.					
n.					
o.					
p.					
q.					
r.					
s.					
t.					
u.					
v.					
w.					
x.					

Page not used.

1. *Omit "00" in the cents columns.*

Statement of Cost of Goods Manufactured
For Year Ended

PROBLEM 21 - 8 ___ , Continued

2. *Omit "00" in the cents columns.*

Income Statement
For Year Ended

3. *Omit "00" in the cents columns.*

Retained Earnings Statement
For Year Ended

4. *Omit "00" in the cents columns.*

Balance Sheet

1. _____

2.

3.

4.

JOURNAL

	DATE		DESCRIPTION	POST. REF.	DEBIT	CREDIT	
1							1
2							2
3							3
4							4
5							5
6							6
7							7
8							8
9							9
10							10
11							11
12							12
13							13
14							14
15							15
16							16
17							17
18							18
19							19
20							20
21							21
22							22
23							23
24							24
25							25
26							26
27							27
28							28
29							29
30							30
31							31
32							32

JOURNAL

	DATE		DESCRIPTION	POST. REF.	DEBIT	CREDIT	
1							1
2							2
3							3
4							4
5							5
6							6
7							7
8							8
9							9
10							10
11							11
12							12
13							13
14							14
15							15
16							16
17							17
18							18
19							19
20							20
21							21
22							22
23							23
24							24
25							25
26							26
27							27
28							28
29							29
30							30
31							31
32							32

1. and 2.

JOB ORDER COST SHEET

Customer _____   Date _____

Address _____   Date wanted _____

_____   Date completed _____

Item _____   Job No. _____

ESTIMATE

Direct Materials		Direct Labor		Summary	
	Amount		Amount		Amount
___ meters at $ ___	_____	___ hours at $ ___	_____	Direct materials	_____
___ meters at ___	_____	___ hours at ___	_____	Direct labor	_____
___ meters at ___	_____	___ hours at ___	_____	Factory overhead	_____
___ meters at ___	_____	___ hours at ___	_____	Total cost	_____
Total	_____	Total	_____		

ACTUAL

Direct Materials			Direct Labor			Summary	
Mat. Req. No.	Description	Amount	Time Ticket No.	Description	Amount	Item	Amount
___	_____	_____	___	_____	_____	Direct materials	_____
___	_____	_____	___	_____	_____	Direct labor	_____
___	_____	_____	___	_____	_____	Factory overhead	_____
___	_____	_____	___	_____	_____	Total cost	_____
Total		_____	Total		_____		

Comments:

Page not used.

1. and 2.

Cash

Bal.	

Prepaid Expenses

Bal.	

Accounts Receivable

Bal.	

Plant Assets

Bal.	

Finished Goods

Bal.	

Accumulated Depreciation—Plant Assets

	Bal.

Work in Process

Bal.	

Accounts Payable

	Bal.

Materials

Bal.	

Wages Payable

Factory Overhead

Common Stock

Bal.

Retained Earnings

Bal.

Selling Expenses

Sales

Administrative Expenses

Cost of Goods Sold

3. *Omit "00" in the cents columns.*

Income Statement

For Month Ended

4. *Omit "00" in the cents columns.*

Retained Earnings Statement

For Month Ended

5. *Omit "00" in the cents columns.*

Balance Sheet

2.

JOURNAL

	DATE		DESCRIPTION	POST. REF.	DEBIT	CREDIT	
1							1
2							2
3							3
4							4
5							5
6							6
7							7
8							8
9							9
10							10
11							11
12							12
13							13
14							14
15							15
16							16
17							17
18							18
19							19
20							20
21							21
22							22
23							23
24							24
25							25
26							26
27							27
28							28
29							29
30							30
31							31
32							32

JOURNAL

	DATE		DESCRIPTION	POST. REF.	DEBIT	CREDIT	
1							1
2							2
3							3
4							4
5							5
6							6
7							7
8							8
9							9
10							10
11							11
12							12
13							13
14							14
15							15
16							16
17							17
18							18
19							19
20							20
21							21
22							22
23							23
24							24
25							25
26							26
27							27
28							28
29							29
30							30
31							31
32							32

Name _____

1. and 2.

GENERAL LEDGER

Cash

Bal.

Accounts Receivable

Bal.

Finished Goods

Bal.

Work in Process

Bal.

Materials

Bal.

Plant Assets

Bal.

Accumulated Depreciation — Plant Assets

Bal.

Accounts Payable

Bal.

Wages Payable

Bal.

Capital Stock

Bal.

Retained Earnings

	Bal.

Sales

	Bal.

Cost of Goods Sold

Bal.	

Factory Overhead

Bal.	

Selling and Administrative Expenses

Bal.	

FINISHED GOODS LEDGER

Commodity _____

Bal.	

Commodity _____

Bal.	

Commodity _____

Bal.	

COST LEDGER

Job No. _____

Bal.	

Job No. _____

Job No. _____

MATERIALS LEDGER

Material _____

Bal.	

Material _____

Bal.	

Material _____

Bal.	

3. *Omit "00" in the cents columns.*

Trial Balance

4.

Finished Goods Ledger

Cost Ledger

Materials Ledger

5. *Omit "00" in the cents columns.*

Income Statement
For Two Months Ended

Page not used.

1. and 3.

MINI-CASE 22, Concluded

2.

	1994			1993		
	DIRECT LABOR COST	MACHINE HOURS		DIRECT LABOR COST	MACHINE HOURS	
Actual overhead						
Applied overhead						
(Over) underapplied overhead						

	1992			1991		
	DIRECT LABOR COST	MACHINE HOURS		DIRECT LABOR COST	MACHINE HOURS	
Actual overhead						
Applied overhead						
(Over) underapplied overhead						

	1990	
	DIRECT LABOR COST	MACHINE HOURS
Actual overhead		
Applied overhead		
(Over) underapplied overhead		

1. and 2.

ACCOUNT   *Work in Process—Department____*   ACCOUNT NO.

DATE	ITEM	POST. REF.	DEBIT	CREDIT	BALANCE DEBIT	BALANCE CREDIT

1., 2. and 3.

1. _____

3.

2.

Cost of Production Report—Department _____

For Month Ended

1.

JOURNAL

	DATE		DESCRIPTION	POST. REF.	DEBIT	CREDIT	
1							1
2							2
3							3
4							4
5							5
6							6
7							7
8							8
9							9
10							10
11							11
12							12
13							13
14							14
15							15
16							16
17							17
18							18
19							19
20							20
21							21
22							22
23							23
24							24
25							25
26							26
27							27
28							28
29							29
30							30
31							31
32							32

JOURNAL

	DATE		DESCRIPTION	POST. REF.	DEBIT	CREDIT	
1							1
2							2
3							3
4							4
5							5
6							6
7							7
8							8
9							9
10							10
11							11
12							12
13							13
14							14
15							15
16							16
17							17
18							18
19							19
20							20
21							21
22							22
23							23
24							24
25							25
26							26
27							27
28							28
29							29
30							30
31							31
32							32

Name _____

JOURNAL   PAGE _____

	DATE		DESCRIPTION	POST. REF.	DEBIT	CREDIT	
1							1
2							2
3							3
4							4
5							5
6							6
7							7
8							8
9							9
10							10
11							11
12							12
13							13
14							14
15							15
16							16
17							17
18							18
19							19
20							20
21							21
22							22
23							23
24							24
25							25
26							26
27							27
28							28
29							29
30							30
31							31
32							32

2.

Name _____

PROBLEM 23 - 4 ___

Cost of Production Report—Department 2

For Month Ended

637

JOURNAL

PAGE _____

	DATE		DESCRIPTION	POST. REF.	DEBIT	CREDIT	
1							1
2							2
3							3
4							4
5							5
6							6
7							7
8							8
9							9
10							10
11							11
12							12
13							13
14							14
15							15
16							16
17							17
18							18
19							19
20							20
21							21
22							22
23							23
24							24
25							25
26							26
27							27
28							28
29							29
30							30
31							31
32							32

PROBLEM 23 - 5 ___ , Concluded

JOURNAL

PAGE

	DATE		DESCRIPTION	POST. REF.	DEBIT	CREDIT	
1							1
2							2
3							3
4							4
5							5
6							6
7							7
8							8
9							9
10							10
11							11
12							12
13							13
14							14
15							15
16							16
17							17
18							18
19							19
20							20
21							21
22							22
23							23
24							24
25							25
26							26
27							27
28							28
29							29
30							30
31							31
32							32

Name _____

PROBLEM 23 - 6 ___

1. *Omit "00" in the cents columns.*

Income Statement

For Month Ended

2. *Omit "00" in the cents columns.*

Retained Earnings Statement

For Month Ended

3. *Omit "00" in the cents columns.*

Balance Sheet

1. _____

2.

Cost of Production Report—Department ____

For Month Ended

Name _____

1. _____

PROBLEM 23 - 8 ___ , Continued

2. and 3.

4.

Page not used.

1., 2., and 3. _____

4.

5.

6.

1.

IPC INC.

Cost of Production Report—Polishing Department

For Month Ended June 30, 19—

2., 3., 4. and 5.

Cost	Fixed Cost	Variable Cost	Mixed Cost
a.			
b.			
c.			
d.			
e.			
f.			
g.			
h.			
i.			
j.			
k.			
l.			
m.			
n.			
o.			
p.			
q.			
r.			
s.			
t.			

Page not used.

1. *Omit "00" in the cents columns.*

	FIXED COSTS	VARIABLE COSTS	

2. through 8.

1. _____
_____
_____
_____
_____
_____

2. _____
_____
_____
_____
_____
_____
_____
_____

3. Sales and Costs

Units of Sales

4. _____
_____
_____

Page not used.

1. Sales and Costs

Units of Sales

2.a. _____

b. _____

Sales and Costs

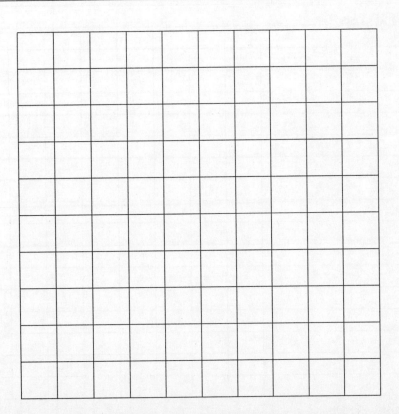

Units of Sales

3. Sales and Costs

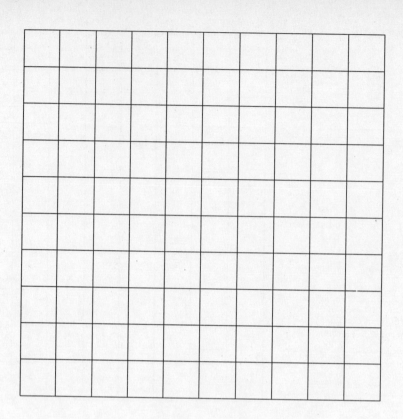

Units of Sales

4.a. _____

b. _____

Sales and Costs

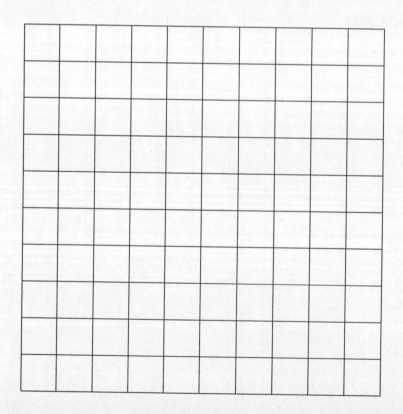

Units of Sales

1. and 2. _____

Name _____

1. *Omit "00" in the cents columns.*

Estimated Income Statement

For Year Ending December 31, 1993

2. and 3.

_____

_____

_____

_____

_____

_____

_____

_____

_____

_____

_____

_____

4.

Sales and Costs

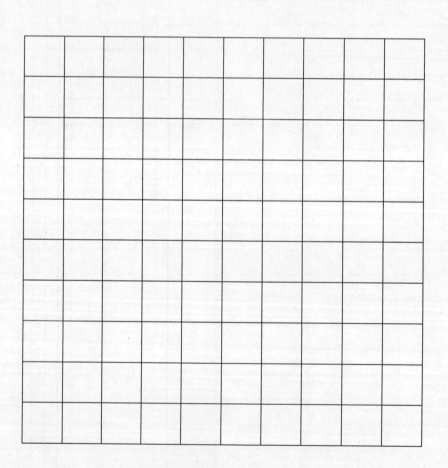

Units of Sales

5. and 6.

Page not used.

1., 2., 3., 4. and 5.

Name _____

1.

	UNIT BUDGETED SALES		ACTUAL SALES FOR NINE MONTHS	INCREASE (DECREASE)	
	YEAR	NINE MONTHS		AMOUNT	PERCENT
Product ___:					
East					
Central					
West					
Product ___:					
East					
Central					
West					

2.

	1993 BUDGETED UNITS	PERCENTAGE INCREASE (DECREASE)	1994 BUDGETED UNITS
Product ___:			
East			
Central			
West			
Product ___:			
East			
Central			
West			

3. *Omit "00" in the cents columns.*

Sales Budget

For Year Ending December 31, 1994

PRODUCT AND AREA	UNIT SALES VOLUME	UNIT SELLING PRICE	TOTAL SALES	
Product ___:				
East				
Central				
West				
Total				
Product ___:				
East				
Central				
West				
Total				
Total revenue from sales				

1. *Omit "00" in the cents columns.*

Sales Budget
For Month Ending May 31, 19–

PRODUCT AND AREA	UNIT SALES VOLUME	UNIT SELLING PRICE	TOTAL SALES	

2. *Omit "00" in the cents columns.*

Production Budget
For Month Ending May 31, 19–

	UNITS		
	PRODUCT ___	PRODUCT ___	

3. *Omit "00" in the cents columns.*

Direct Materials Purchases Budget
For Month Ending May 31, 19–

	DIRECT MATERIALS			

4. *Omit "00" in the cents columns.*

Direct Labor Cost Budget
For Month Ending

	DEPARTMENT ___	DEPARTMENT ___	DEPARTMENT ___

1. *Omit "00" in the cents columns.*

Sales Budget
For Month Ending

PRODUCT	UNIT SALES VOLUME	UNIT SELLING PRICE	TOTAL SALES

2. *Omit "00" in the cents columns.*

Production Budget		
For Month Ending		

	UNITS	
	PRODUCT ___	PRODUCT ___

3. *Omit "00" in the cents columns.*

Direct Materials Purchases Budget
For Month Ending

	DIRECT MATERIALS			TOTAL

4. *Omit "00" in the cents columns.*

Direct Labor Cost Budget
For Month Ending

	DEPARTMENT ___	DEPARTMENT ___	DEPARTMENT ___	TOTAL

5. *Omit "00" in the cents columns.*

Factory Overhead Cost Budget

For Month Ending

6. *Omit "00" in the cents columns.*

Cost of Goods Sold Budget

For Month Ending

Computations

7. *Omit "00" in the cents columns.*

Operating Expenses Budget

For Month Ending

8. *Omit "00" in the cents columns.*

Budgeted Income Statement										
For Month Ending										

Page not used.

1. *Omit "00" in the cents columns.*

Cash Budget

For Three Months Ending June 30, 19__

	APRIL	MAY	JUNE

Computations

2.

1. *Omit "00" in the cents columns.*

Budgeted Income Statement

For Year Ending December 31, 19–

PROBLEM 25 - 5 ____ , Continued

2. *Omit "00" in the cents columns.*

Budgeted Balance Sheet

December 31, 1994

Computations

Page not used.

a. _____

_____

_____

_____

_____

_____

_____

_____

_____

_____

_____

_____

_____

_____

_____

_____

_____

_____

_____

_____

b. _____

_____

_____

_____

_____

_____

_____

_____

_____

_____

_____

_____

_____

_____

_____

_____

_____

_____

_____

c.

Standard Factory Overhead Cost Variance Report—Department _____
For Month Ending

Productive capacity for the month

Actual production for the month

	BUDGET	ACTUAL	VARIANCES	
			FAVORABLE	UNFAVORABLE

Page not used.

1. *Omit "00" in the cents columns.*

Factory Overhead Cost Budget— _____ *Department*
For Month Ending _____

Percent of productive capacity					
Machine hours					
Budgeted factory overhead					

PROBLEM 25 - 8 ___ , Concluded

2. *Omit "00" in the cents columns.*

Factory Overhead Cost Variance Report— _____ *Department*
For Month Ending

Productive capacity for the month

Actual production for the month

	BUDGET	ACTUAL	VARIANCES	
			FAVORABLE	UNFAVORABLE

1.

PALL COMPANY
Factory Overhead Cost Variance Report
For Month Ending August 31, 19—

Productive capacity for the month (100%)
Standard for amount produced during the month

	BUDGET	ACTUAL	VARIANCES	
			FAVORABLE	UNFAVORABLE

2., 3., 4. and 5.

1. *Omit "00" in the cents columns.*

Estimated Income Statement											
For Year Ending											

2.

Page not used.

Name _____

PROBLEM 26 - 2 ___

1. *Omit "00" in the cents columns.*

Income Statement

For Month Ended

	DEPARTMENT	DEPARTMENT	OTHER DEPARTMENTS	TOTAL

2.

1. Omit "00" in the cents column.

Income Statement

For Year Ended

DEPARTMENT ___

DEPARTMENT ___

TOTAL

TOTAL

DEPARTMENT ___

DEPARTMENT ___

2.

3.

The 10-column work sheet form for Problem 26-4A or 26-4B is on page 781.
1. *Omit "00" in the cents columns.*

Divisional Income Statements

For Year Ended _____

	DIVISION ____	DIVISION ____	DIVISION ____
Sales			
Cost of goods sold			
Gross profit			
Operating expenses			
Operating income			

2. and 3.

_____
_____
_____
_____
_____
_____
_____
_____
_____
_____
_____
_____
_____
_____
_____
_____
_____
_____
_____
_____
_____
_____
_____
_____

1.

2. *Omit "00" in the cents columns.*

Estimated Income Statements

For Year Ending

	PROPOSAL 1	PROPOSAL 2	PROPOSAL 3

PROBLEM 26 - 6 ___ , Concluded

3., 4. and 5.

1. _____

2. and 3.
_____

_____

_____

_____

_____

_____

_____

_____

_____

_____

_____

_____

_____

_____

_____

_____

_____

_____

_____

_____

_____

_____

_____

_____

_____

_____

_____

_____

_____

_____

_____

_____

_____

_____

_____

_____

_____

_____

1. *Omit "00" in the cents columns.*

Divisional Income Statements																	
For Year Ended																	
	DIVISION ___						DIVISION ___					
Sales												
Cost of goods sold												
Gross profit												
Operating expenses												
Operating income												

2., 3. and 4.

PROBLEM 26 - 8 ___ , Concluded

1.

2. *Omit "00" in the cents columns.*

Division ____

	1994	1993	1992
Divisional operating income			
Minimum amount of operating income:			
Residual income			

Division ____

	1994	1993	1992
Divisional operating income			
Minimum amount of operating income:			
Residual income			

3.

	DIVISION SALES	TOTAL INDUSTRY SALES	MARKET SHARE
Division ____ :			
1994			
1993			
1992			
Division ____ :			
1994			
1993			
1992			

4. and 5.

1. and 2.

3. *Omit "00" in the cents columns.*

Divisional Income Statements

For Year Ended December 31, 19—

	DIVISION ____	DIVISION ____	TOTAL

4. and 5.

Name _____

PROBLEM 26 - 10 ___ , Concluded

725

Page not used.

1., 2., 3., 4. and 5.

Name _____

1. *Omit "00" in the cents columns.*

Proposal to Operate Warehouse

2.

3. *Omit "00" in the cents columns.*

1. *Omit "00" in the cents columns.*

Proposal to Replace Machine

2.

1. *Omit "00" in the cents columns.*

Proposals for Sales Promotion Campaign

	PRODUCT ___	PRODUCT ___

2.

Page not used.

Name _____

1. *Omit "00" in the cents columns.*

Proposal To Process Product ____ Further

2.

Page not used.

1. *Omit "00" in the cents columns.*

Proposal To Process Product ____ Further _____

2. _____

Page not used.

1. _____
_____
_____

2. _____
_____
_____
_____
_____
_____
_____
_____
_____
_____
_____
_____
_____
_____
_____
_____

3. _____
_____
_____
_____
_____
_____
_____
_____
_____
_____
_____
_____
_____
_____
_____
_____
_____
_____
_____

4.

5.

6.a. *Omit "00" in the cents columns.*

Proposal To Sell to

b.

1., 2. and 3.

1.a. _____

_____

_____

_____

_____

b.

Year	Present Value of $1 at _____%	Net Cash Flow		Present Value of Net Cash Flow	
		Project _____	Project _____	Project _____	Project _____
1					
2					
3					
4					
5					
Total					
Amount to be invested					
Net present value					

2. _____

_____

_____

_____

_____

_____

_____

_____

_____

_____

_____

_____

_____

_____

_____

_____

_____

_____

_____

_____

1.a. _____
_____
_____
_____
_____

b.

Year	Present Value of $1 at _____ %	Net Cash Flow		Present Value of Net Cash Flow	
		Project _____	Project _____	Project _____	Project _____
1					
2					
3					
4					
5					
Total					
Amount to be invested					
Net present value					

2. _____
_____
_____
_____
_____
_____
_____
_____
_____
_____
_____
_____
_____
_____
_____
_____

1. Proposal (Project) _____:

Year	Present Value of $1 at _____%	Net Cash Flow	Present Value of Net Cash Flow
1			
2			
3			
Total			
Amount to be invested			
Net present value			

Proposal (Project) _____:

Year	Present Value of $1 at _____%	Net Cash Flow	Present Value of Net Cash Flow
1			
2			
3			
Total			
Amount to be invested			
Net present value			

Proposal (Project) _____:

Year	Present Value of $1 at _____%	Net Cash Flow	Present Value of Net Cash Flow
1			
2			
3			
Total			
Amount to be invested			
Net present value			

2.

3.

1.a.

Year	Present Value of $1 at _____ %	Net Cash Flow		Present Value of Net Cash Flow	
		Project _____	Project _____	Project _____	Project _____
1					
2					
3					
4					
Total					
Amount to be invested					
Net present value					

b.

_____
_____
_____
_____
_____
_____
_____
_____
_____
_____
_____
_____
_____
_____
_____
_____
_____
_____
_____
_____
_____
_____
_____
_____

2.a.

b.

3.

Name _____

1.

Year	Present Value of $1 at 15%	Net Cash Flow		Present Value of Net Cash Flow	
		Project _____	Project _____	Project _____	Project _____
1					
2					
3					
4					
5					
6					
Total					
Amount to be invested					
Net present value					

2.

Year	Present Value of $1 at 15%	Net Cash Flow		Present Value of Net Cash Flow	
		Project _____	Project _____	Project _____	Project _____
1					
2					
3					
4					
Total					
Amount to be invested					
Net present value					

3.

Name _____

1. _____

PROBLEM 28 - 6 ___ , Continued

2.

3.

Proposal	Cash Payback Period	Average Rate of Return	Accept for Further Analysis	Reject
A				
B				
C				
D				
E				
F				

4. Proposal A:

Year	Present Value of $1 at 10%	Net Cash Flow	Present Value of Net Cash Flow
1			
2			
3			
4			
5			
Total			
Amount to be invested			
Net present value			

PROBLEM 28 - 6 _____ , Continued

Proposal C:

Year	Present Value of $1 at 10%	Net Cash Flow	Present Value of Net Cash Flow
1			
2			
3			
4			
5			
Total			
Amount to be invested			
Net present value			

Proposal E:

Year	Present Value of $1 at 10%	Net Cash Flow	Present Value of Net Cash Flow
1			
2			
3			
4			
5			
Total			
Amount to be invested			
Net present value			

Name _____

5.

6.

7.

8.

Name _____

MINI-CASE 28

1. _____

2.

Year	Present Value of $1 at 12%	Net Cash Flow		Present Value of Net Cash Flow	
		Project G	Project H	Project G	Project H
1					
2					
3					
4					
Total					
Amount to be invested					
Net present value					

_____
_____
_____
_____
_____
_____
_____
_____
_____
_____
_____
_____
_____
_____
_____
_____
_____
_____
_____
_____
_____
_____

1. *The 10-column work sheet form is on page 782.*
2. *Omit "00" in the cents columns.*

GUNN MANUFACTURING INC.
Statement of Cost of Goods Manufactured
For Year Ended December 31, 19—

PROBLEM F - 1, Continued

3. *Omit "00" in the cents columns.*

GUNN MANUFACTURING INC.

Income Statement

For Year Ended December 31, 19—

762

4. *Omit "00" in the cents columns.*

GUNN MANUFACTURING INC.

Retained Earnings Statement

For Year Ended December 31, 19—

5. *Omit "00" in the cents columns.*

GUNN MANUFACTURING INC.

Balance Sheet

December 31, 19—

PROBLEM F - 1, Concluded

GUNN MANUFACTURING INC.

Balance Sheet (continued)

December 31, 19—

PROBLEM F - 1, Concluded

764

1. *Omit "00" in the cents columns.*

PYLE CO.

Statement of Cost of Goods Manufactured

For Year Ended December 31, 19—

2. *Omit "00" in the cents columns.*

PYLE CO.

Income Statement

For Year Ended December 31, 19—

3. *Omit "00" in the cents columns.*

PYLE CO.

Retained Earnings Statement

For Year Ended December 31, 19—

4. *Omit "00" in the cents columns.*

PYLE CO.

Balance Sheet

December 31, 19—

PYLE CO.

Balance Sheet (continued)

December 31, 19—

1. and 2.

JOURNAL

	DATE		DESCRIPTION	POST. REF.	DEBIT	CREDIT	
1							1
2							2
3							3
4							4
5							5
6							6
7							7
8							8
9							9
10							10
11							11
12							12
13							13
14							14
15							15
16							16
17							17
18							18
19							19
20							20
21							21
22							22
23							23
24							24
25							25
26							26
27							27
28							28
29							29
30							30
31							31
32							32

PROBLEM F - 3, Concluded

JOURNAL

PAGE

	DATE		DESCRIPTION	POST. REF.	DEBIT	CREDIT	
1							1
2							2
3							3
4							4
5							5
6							6
7							7
8							8
9							9
10							10
11							11
12							12
13							13
14							14
15							15
16							16
17							17
18							18
19							19
20							20
21							21
22							22
23							23
24							24
25							25
26							26
27							27
28							28
29							29
30							30
31							31
32							32

1. *Omit "00" in the cents columns.*

MAYE CO.

Statement of Cost of Goods Manufactured

For Year Ended December 31, 19—

PROBLEM F - 4, Concluded

2., 3. and 4.

JOURNAL

	DATE		DESCRIPTION	POST. REF.	DEBIT	CREDIT	
1							1
2							2
3							3
4							4
5							5
6							6
7							7
8							8
9							9
10							10
11							11
12							12
13							13
14							14
15							15
16							16
17							17
18							18
19							19
20							20
21							21
22							22
23							23
24							24
25							25
26							26
27							27
28							28
29							29
30							30
31							31
32							32

Name _____

JOURNAL   PAGE _____

	DATE		DESCRIPTION	POST. REF.	DEBIT	CREDIT	
1							1
2							2
3							3
4							4
5							5
6							6
7							7
8							8
9							9
10							10
11							11
12							12
13							13
14							14
15							15
16							16
17							17
18							18
19							19
20							20
21							21
22							22
23							23
24							24
25							25
26							26
27							27
28							28
29							29
30							30
31							31
32							32

JOURNAL

PAGE

	DATE		DESCRIPTION	POST. REF.	DEBIT	CREDIT	
1							1
2							2
3							3
4							4
5							5
6							6
7							7
8							8
9							9
10							10
11							11
12							12
13							13
14							14
15							15
16							16
17							17
18							18
19							19
20							20
21							21
22							22
23							23
24							24
25							25
26							26
27							27
28							28
29							29
30							30
31							31
32							32

Name _____

JOURNAL

PAGE _____

	DATE		DESCRIPTION	POST. REF.	DEBIT	CREDIT	
1							1
2							2
3							3
4							4
5							5
6							6
7							7
8							8
9							9
10							10
11							11
12							12
13							13
14							14
15							15
16							16
17							17
18							18
19							19
20							20
21							21
22							22
23							23
24							24
25							25
26							26
27							27
28							28
29							29
30							30
31							31
32							32

	DATE		DESCRIPTION	POST. REF.	DEBIT	CREDIT	
1							1
2							2
3							3
4							4
5							5
6							6
7							7
8							8
9							9
10							10
11							11
12							12
13							13
14							14
15							15
16							16
17							17
18							18
19							19
20							20
21							21
22							22
23							23
24							24
25							25
26							26
27							27
28							28
29							29
30							30
31							31
32							32

Name _____

JOURNAL

	DATE		DESCRIPTION	POST. REF.	DEBIT	CREDIT	
1							1
2							2
3							3
4							4
5							5
6							6
7							7
8							8
9							9
10							10
11							11
12							12
13							13
14							14
15							15
16							16
17							17
18							18
19							19
20							20
21							21
22							22
23							23
24							24
25							25
26							26
27							27
28							28
29							29
30							30
31							31
32							32

JOURNAL

PAGE

	DATE		DESCRIPTION	POST. REF.	DEBIT	CREDIT	
1							1
2							2
3							3
4							4
5							5
6							6
7							7
8							8
9							9
10							10
11							11
12							12
13							13
14							14
15							15
16							16
17							17
18							18
19							19
20							20
21							21
22							22
23							23
24							24
25							25
26							26
27							27
28							28
29							29
30							30
31							31
32							32

STATEMENT OF COST OF GOODS MANUFACTURED		INCOME STATEMENT		BALANCE SHEET	
DEBIT	CREDIT	DEBIT	CREDIT	DEBIT	CREDIT

GLENN MANUFACTURING INC.

Work Sheet

For Year Ended December 31, 19—

ACCOUNT TITLE	TRIAL BALANCE		ADJUSTMENTS	
	DEBIT	CREDIT	DEBIT	CREDIT
Cash	2 9 7 5 0			
Accounts Receivable	4 9 2 5 0			
Allowance for Doubtful Accounts		9 0 0		
Finished Goods	5 5 6 0 0			
Work in Process	3 2 1 0 0			
Direct Materials	4 2 0 0 0			
Prepaid Expenses (Controlling)	1 0 0 0 0			
Land	5 0 0 0 0			
Factory Buildings	2 8 0 0 0 0			
Accumulated Depr.—Factory Buildings		9 0 0 0 0		
Factory Equipment	1 7 2 8 5 0			
Accumulated Depr.—Factory Equipment		9 7 9 5 0		
Office Equipment	3 0 0 0 0			
Accumulated Depr.—Office Equipment		1 0 0 0 0		
Accounts Payable		4 0 4 0 0		
Wages Payable				
Common Stock ($20 par)		3 0 0 0 0 0		
Retained Earnings		1 2 8 4 5 0		
Dividends	2 0 0 0 0			
Income Summary				
Manufacturing Summary				
Sales		6 8 8 5 0 0		
Direct Materials Purchases	1 9 7 0 0 0			
Direct Labor	1 7 8 6 0 0			
Factory Overhead (Controlling)	6 5 1 5 6			
Selling Expenses (Controlling)	1 6 2 7 5			
Administrative Expenses (Controlling)	6 8 8 2 5			
Interest Expense	3 5 0 0			
	1 3 3 4 2 0 0	1 3 3 4 2 0 0		
Cost of Goods Manufactured				
Net Income				